# GREATER NOTTINGHAM

# GREATER NOTTINGHAM

## Geoffrey Oldfield

Book Guild Publishing

Sussex, England

First published in Great Britain in 2006 by
The Book Guild Ltd
Pavilion View
19 New Road
Brighton, East Sussex
BN1 1UF

Typesetting in Times by
MRM Graphics Ltd, Winslow, Buckinghamshire

Printed and bound in Singapore under the supervision of MRM Graphics Ltd, Winslow, Bucks

A catalogue record for this book is available from
The British Library.

ISBN 1 84624 051 4

# Contents

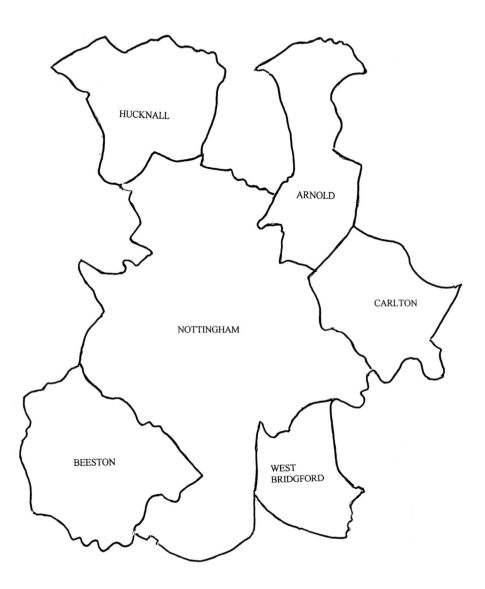

City of Nottingham and the five adjoining former urban districts.

# Introduction

When in 1949 he wrote his book 'Nottingham Through 500 Years', Duncan Gray entitled Chapter X 'Greater Nottingham'. He used this term to describe the growth of Nottingham in 1877. This had been achieved by a Boundary Extension Act which added to the relatively small area of the borough the adjoining parishes to form a town of 10,935 acres. The town continued to grow in population, as did five parishes which had contiguous boundaries with the city, as it became in 1897. In 1895, these five parishes were granted the status of urban districts which were created by the Local Government Act 1894. Other areas adjacent to the town were included in new rural districts.

Although in the first decade of the twentieth century the city continued to grow in population, the urban districts grew at a faster rate. This caused concern to the members of the City Council who feared loss of trade and rates to the other areas. A Bill was therefore promoted in 1912 to obtain another Boundary Extension Act. This sought to include the Urban District Councils, as well as parts of the Rural District Councils. The objective was informally described from this time onwards creating a Greater Nottingham, governed by one local authority, the City Council.

The Bill was not pursued at that time but was reintroduced in 1920. The scheme did not obtain Government approval, but the City Council did not abandon the idea. A subsequent extension was granted in 1935 and another one in 1952. In both cases, the areas added were part of rural districts where the City Council had acquired land on which it built council houses.

The next 22 years saw a prolonged debate on what shape local authorities areas should be and various proposals included some suggestions which might have brought about a Greater Nottingham City Council. However, in 1974, the Government radically altered local government by abolishing urban and rural districts and boroughs, including all-purpose county boroughs, of which Nottingham was one. In their place, as far as Nottinghamshire was concerned, were substituted a new county council with wider powers over the whole country, with eight second-tier district councils. Nottingham was one of these and it lost some of its functions to the County Council. These were restored to it in 1998 when it became a unitary authority. For the time being at least, Nottingham City's dream of a Greater Nottingham Council must be regarded as just that.

Yet paradoxically, the twentieth century has seen the emergence of it as a topographical reality. The growth of transport by motor vehicles, the transformation of industry, new technology in communications and increases in standards of living overall have resulted in the term having a new validity.

Exactly where this Greater Nottingham lies is to some extent a matter of debate. For the purpose of this book, I have taken it to mean the City of Nottingham and the five urban districts as they were up to 1974. This can, I consider, be justified by regarding this as a largely built-up area. It can perhaps be argued that such places as Ruddington and Burton Joyce are equally part of Greater Nottingham. In some respects, they probably are and the term has to be regarded as flexible.

In this book, I have tried to illustrate the way in which my defined area has grown throughout the twentieth century. To do this, I have photographed the areas as they were at the beginning of a new century to show the changing pattern of the built environment in each of the six constituents. I have tried to show the variety of changes in styles and functions which together illustrate 'Greater Nottingham' at the beginning of the twenty-first century and which is entirely a growth of the previous century.

# City of Nottingham

The 1901 census showed that the population of the City of Nottingham that year was 240,000 people living in 55,790 houses. It had been granted the status of City four years earlier in recognition of the way in which it had in the nineteenth century grown from a small borough to become one of the major provincial towns. This growth was measured not only by the increase in population – almost tenfold in the hundred years – but also by an expansion of its area. In the 1871 census, the population was 86,621 but this was contained in the same 1,933 acres which had been unchanged since early medieval times. Ten years later, the population was 186,575 and the area 10,935 acres. These increases had been achieved mainly by the passing of a Borough Extension Act of 1877. This brought within the borough boundaries the whole of five adjoining parishes, part of another one and what had been a non-parochial district. The five parishes were Basford, Bulwell, Lenton, Radford and Sneinton, together with the northern part of Wilford and the liberties of the Castle, which included Nottingham Park.

The growth of population had been caused by the influx of people from outside the town and from other counties, due to increasing industrialisation. Hosiery in the eighteenth century, followed by lace in the second half of the nineteenth century and other industries in the last quarter had attracted the growing population of England from less industrialised areas.

The distribution of the 240,000 people in 1901 was far from uniform throughout the City. Under half the population, 108,000, lived in the 1,933 acres of the old borough, whilst the remaining 132,000 occupied the 9,000 acres in the former parishes brought in in 1877. This trend was to continue in the first decade of the twentieth century with new houses being built in the districts away from the City centre. This was assisted by developments in public transport. Some slowing down on house-building and construction generally took place after 1910 and during the 1914–18 War such work virtually ceased.

Between 1920 and 1939, considerable changes took place in the City. The City Council started building houses to let for the working classes, mainly on the outer districts. More than 17,000 had been built by 1939, when war again stopped all construction not directly needed for war purposes. The 1920s and 1930s also witnessed other changes – demolition of the worst insanitary and overcrowded areas in the old Borough area, improvements in sewage disposal and provision of

1

electricity, the building of new roads to meet the increase in motor vehicles, new methods of public transport, the creation of better amenities such as parks, baths and libraries, the building of the prestigious University College and the Council House and the acquisition of Wollaton Park with its Elizabethan mansion. The building of some council houses outside the City boundary led to a successful application for extension into adjoining rural areas, bringing the total acreage to 16,172.

The end of the War in 1945 left Nottingham with a legacy of no new buildings for the previous six years and the deterioration of existing properties, especially older houses and industrial buildings. For the first 10 years after the War, priority was given to building houses, mainly by the City Council, and this led to a further extension of the boundaries by bringing in Clifton. This increased the total acreage to its present 18,304 acres. The next 10 years or so saw a gradual improvement of the City by resuming clearance schemes and by starting to remedy some of the problems caused by the great increase in road traffic. This period also saw the erection of high-rise flats and commercial buildings and the loss of some of the City's older historic heritage.

The last quarter of the twentieth century saw the physical appearance of the City change in a far greater way than in any previous period. Two large-scale redevelopments of mainly residential areas, St Anns and Meadows, were accompanied by a flight of manufacturing industries, to be replaced by other economic sectors such as leisure and finance. Two covered shopping malls altered the retail shape of the City, as did the advent of supermarkets and the loss of smaller shops. The new Playhouse Theatre in the 1960s was followed in 1970 by the erection of a Concert Hall, whilst the Queen's Medical Centre replaced the existing hospitals in the City centre. The expansion of further education colleges was accompanied by the creation and expansion of a new University.

The last few years of the century saw perhaps the most dramatic changes of all. The redevelopment of the General Hospital site, not yet completed; the regeneration of the railway lands and the Nottingham canal sides; the redevelopment of the former Boots industrial complex on London Road; the refurbishment of the Lace Market; and the demolition of the Evening Post offices leading to a new leisure complex were accompanied right at the end of the century by the building of the National Ice Centre. The year 2004 also saw the construction of the terminal of the new tramway, Nottingham Express Transit. This, like many of the buildings erected in the twentieth century, will further enhance the concept of Greater Nottingham.

An important addition to the City's public transport opened the twentieth century. The electric tramways had this depot on Mansfield Road.

The Midland Station on Carrington Street designed by A. E. Lambert was opened in 1904, replacing a smaller one on Station Street.

Dated 1902 on its pediment, this building at the junction of Talbot Street and Wollaton Street was erected as livery stables but has had several other different uses since.

The superstore on Lower Parliament Street was originally occupied by a motor car firm. The building was later called Lombard House.

The earliest plans for new houses in 1901 included several schemes in Bulwell, including these on Henrietta Street.

More spacious houses with gardens in a secluded area at Sherwood were built about the same time on Burlington Road.

A new building for the Gordon Boys Home was opened in 1904 on Cranmer Street.

A new Albert Hall on Circus Street was opened in 1907 to replace an earlier one destroyed by fire. It was designed by A. E. Lambert who was the architect for the new Midland Station.

This large tenement factory block on Castle Boulevard extends from Maid Marian Way to Castle Road. When built in 1907, the road was known as Lenton Boulevard but was changed shortly afterwards.

The Liberal Club on Highbury Road, Bulwell has a number of foundation stones which are dated 1908.

Now known as Westminster Buildings, this large block of offices and shops is on Upper Parliament Street and Wollaton Street. This part of Parliament Street had been widened and new buildings erected from 1897.

One of the first cinemas to be built in the City was the Goldsmith Street Picture House opened in 1911 and called at first Pringle's Picture Palace. It later became the forerunner of Nottingham Playhouse and is now a public house.

The names of the streets between Sneinton Boulevard and Colwick Road include several which were influenced by places involved in the Boer War. This part of Sneinton was largely developed during the Edwardian era and in 1912 St Christopher's Church was built. The vicarage in Sneinton Boulevard is an attractive building with Arts and Crafts movement details.

The Olive Tree Book Shop at the corner of Mansfield Road and Broxtowe was opened in 1911 as a branch bank of the Nottingham and Notts. Banking Company, later Westminster Bank. Its external appearance has been altered since it ceased to be used as a bank.

Another bank built about the same time was the London City and Midland Bank at the corner of Bath Street and Longden Street, later the Midland Bank. Now an architect's office, the external appearance is little altered.

The western end of Upper Parliament Street was widened at the end of the nineteenth century. New buildings were gradually erected on the cleared sites, including the highly decorative shop for the Nottingham Co-operative Society, which was opened in 1916.

Cinemas continued to be built, especially in the outer suburbs, after 1910. This one on Vernon Road was completed in 1915. Known as the Vernon Cinema, the building is still largely unchanged externally although it is now used for industrial purposes.

One of the few permanent buildings erected during the First World War was on King's Meadow Road in the Meadows. Built for an engineering firm, Cammell Laird's, it became a munitions factory, the National Projectile Factory. With later additions, it became the Royal Ordnance factory and is now part of BAE Systems.

An innovation of the end of the 1914–18 war was the encouragement and financial assistance by the government to local authorities to build houses for the working classes. Nottingham undertook this by building some 17,000 houses by 1939. Some of the earliest were on the Sherwood Estate built on garden city lines. These houses on Perry Road were designed especially to give an attractive front on a main road.

The former Elite Cinema on Upper Parliament Street was built in 1921 to a design by a London firm of architects, Adamson and Kinns. Its impressive exterior of glazed terracotta with niches containing emblematic figures was complemented internally by a foyer, lifts, cafes and restaurants, one of which could be converted to a ballroom. It ceased as a cinema in 1977, followed by a period as a bingo hall. Its present use as a nightclub respects much of the original interior.

The period 1920 to 1939 saw a considerable improvement in Nottingham's appearance. One aspect of this was the building of libraries by the City Council, mainly in the areas absorbed into the borough in 1877. One of these is the Vernon Road Library on the edge of Vernon Park at Basford.

Another pioneering activity of the Council was the establishment of the School Medical Service. The classical building with dentelled pediment and quoins was the main clinic on Chaucer Street. It is now part of Nottingham Trent University.

The church notice board of St Augustine of England Roman Catholic Church on Woodborough Road informs us that it was built in 1923 and that the architect was Sidney Brocklesby. Demolitions below have helped to emphasise its Byzantine appearance.

The building of the Sherwood housing estate included a new road, Valley Road, from Daybrook to Basford, opened in 1922. This enabled development at the Basford end on the north side, including this building, No. 536, for what was then the National Provincial Bank. The first floor has a Georgian harmony.

A start on demolishing unhealthy properties in the Carter Gate area had been made before 1914, but further work was postponed during the war. It was resumed in the 1920s and was accompanied by the construction of a new road from Glasshouse Street to London Road. A new tramways depot was built at the junction of Stanhope Street extending along Southwell Road.

The major improvement of the decade was the transfer of the open market to King Edward Street, the creation of the processional way, the demolition of the old Exchange and its replacement by the Council House designed by T. C. Howitt. Although criticised by some at the time and later by Nikolaus Pevsner, it is now recognised as the symbol of Nottingham.

The widening of Friar Lane started in 1924 with the demolition of properties on the north side as far as Granby Street. At the corner with Beastmarket Hill, a new tailor's shop was built in the style which was standard for the owners, including a similar building at the end of Clumber Street.

A few years later, Friar Lane was extended as far as Castle Road by widening and renaming Park Street. The office building No. 84 has a number of classically inspired features.

The buildings on the west side of Lister Gate included a number of offices with multiple tenancies. Some of these were demolished and one of the department stores erected on the cleared sites has ornate Art Deco details on its upper floor.

The extension southward of Lower Parliament Street opened up new sites for development. A commercial building at the corner of Poplar Street was designed to create a curved entrance with Art Deco features.

Clearance of the insanitary and overcrowded houses between Gedling Street and Southwell Road enabled a new Sneinton Wholesale Market for fruit, fish and vegetables to be built. This was done by building several avenues, each with small units. The buildings have Dutch style gable ends and are now used for a variety of purposes as a new wholesale market has been built at Eastcroft.

The Masonic Hall in Goldsmith Street, built in 1924, replaced former buildings. The impressive classical façade has a decorative entrance doorway. The Hall was damaged in an air raid in 1941, but has been skilfully restored.

18

An innovation in housing policy by the City Council in the late 1920s was the building of one bedroom flats in two storeys for elderly tenants. Each block had its own communal laundry and hot water was supplied from a central boiler. This block is on Radbourne Road, Colwick Road.

The thirties saw an extension of the City's inner ring road of boulevards constructed after the borough was extended in 1877. Western Boulevard from Ilkeston Boulevard to Old Basford, part of a housing scheme linked with Valley Road to form an outer ring road. The council houses at the Ilkeston Road end were specially designed in a variety of styles.

The architect of the Council House, T. C. Howitt, designed a new bungalow for himself on Baildon Close, Wollaton Park. It originally had a thatched roof.

An innovative building of 1932 was the office and warehouse known as Viyella House for William Hollins and Company. Its modern appearance was distinguished by extensive use of glass walling.

Built about the same time as Viyella House, the large department store on Long Row and Market Street of Griffin and Spalding contrasted with it by using a classical design.

The popularity of ballroom dancing in the 1920s and 1930s resulted in the building of modern dance halls. Greyfriars Hall on Collin Street later became much better known as the Astoria Ballroom. It has had several changes of name since.

The coming of talking films was followed by the building of new luxury cinemas both in the City centre and the suburbs. Formerly the Aspley Cinema on Nuthall Road, the Commodore International had restaurants, conference and banqueting suites.

The spiritual needs of the expanding suburbs, especially those being built away from older settled areas, called for new churches to be built. One of these was St Margaret on Aspley Lane, opened in 1936.

In the same year, a new church hall for Holy Trinity Church in Trinity Square was built on Colville Street, half a mile away. Most of the houses near the church built in 1841 had been demolished, a fate the church itself suffered in the 1950s.

Another new building in 1936, not far from Holy Trinity Church, was the hostel for the Young Women's Christian Association at the corner of Shakespeare Street and North Sherwood Street. It now provides student accommodation for Nottingham Trent University.

An imposing addition to the skyline in 1938 was the erection of tobacco bonded warehouses on Ilkeston Road, near to John Player's tobacco works at Radford.

As in the 1914–18 War, building work except for essential purposes was suspended during the 1939–45 period. An earlier resumption of council housing was started by the provision of pre-fabricated houses by the Government for local authorities. Nottingham took 1,000 of these temporary bungalows, one of which is still in Luton Close, although the life was said to be 10 years.

The early post-1945 period saw the construction of offices for Government buildings on Chalfont Drive, off Western Boulevard. By 1950, there were seven blocks occupied by 22 departments.

To speed up building of houses, the City Council used a number of different types of non-traditional construction. BISF types were built primarily in factories of the British Iron and Steel Federation and quickly assembled on site.

Further education was given some priority in the 1950s when the Nottingham and District Technical College expanded. The building on Burton Street, now known as the Newton building, is part of Nottingham Trent University.

Maid Marian Way, the City's western inner ring road, was only constructed after a protracted and controversial period of years. Castle Gate, Hounds Gate, Friar Lane, St James Street and Mount Street were divided into two halves by the demolition of properties on the line of the road. New buildings such as this one, at the corner of Friar Lane, were erected when the road was completed.

Beyond the pedestrian subway below Maid Marian Way can be seen the multi-storey car park, hotel and office blocks. Planting of trees and shrubs in the central portion has softened the street scene.

A scheme was carried out at the top of Maid Marian Way and Park Row which included a bus station, shops and car park. This was not a success and only the car park remains. The rest of the site has been redeveloped with offices and a casino.

Maid Marian Way required a complete re-arrangement of the highway system at the bottom of Derby Road. Chapel Bar was closed at its top end and new buildings built on the cleared site from Upper Parliament Street southwards.

The 1950s saw a resumption of the pre-1939 clearance of unhealthy and over-crowded areas. Attention from 1954 onwards concentrated mainly on the former separate parishes brought into the Borough in 1877. A major scheme known as the Denman Street redevelopment in Radford resulted in new dwellings, mainly flats and maisonettes, such as the small complex of Grafton Court near Canning Circus.

A medium rise block of maisonettes in the Denman Street scheme is Highhurst Court. The existing street pattern in the southern triangle between Highhurst Street and Canning Circus was retained but with the addition of trees.

An unusual building at the north end of London Road is the power station built by the Boots Company in the 1950s for its own industrial plant. It now forms part of the district heating scheme.

The Friends Meeting House was built in 1962 on Clarendon Street on the edge of the General Cemetery. It replaced a building on Friar Lane which was demolished.

The early 1960s saw redevelopment on both sides of Mansfield Road. Buildings at the corner of Peachey Street, including a cinema, were demolished and a Midland Design Centre built on the site. After the Centre closed, the building became known as Sandfield House and, for a time, was used for overflow Magistrates Courts. Following a recent renovation and facelift, it is now a Voluntary Action Centre.

On the opposite side of Mansfield Road, York House was built by the City Council and provided offices for some of its staff as well as studios for the BBC.

The demolition of the Black Boy Hotel on Long Row was regretted by many, especially as its replacement was an undistinguished looking shopping row.

Some compensation architecturally came in the shape of Nottingham Playhouse on Circus Street. Designed by Peter Moro and Partners, Pevsner described it as the only modern building of national importance in the City centre.

The second half of the 1960s saw the beginning of considerable changes in the appearance of the City. The interior shown here is of one of the two large shopping malls, Broad Marsh, which was built over former streets and stopped vehicles travelling south from Wheeler Gate.

The closing of the Victoria Station was followed by the demolition of all the buildings between Woodborough Road and Lower Parliament Street, with the exception of the hotel and clock tower. On the site was built Nottingham's other shopping mall, Victoria Centre. The flats built on top of the mall can be seen from the Bath Street rest garden.

Another large-scale change starting in 1967 was the clearance and redevelopment of the St Ann's area, stretching from Mansfield Road to Carlton Road. Most of the properties in this area were demolished and a new suburb created. The new street pattern, with houses in walks and closes, replaced the old one with narrow streets at right angles to the main thoroughfares.

In the old St Ann's, industry and houses adjoined each other. Now, new segregated light industries are separated from houses.

Many of the St Ann's area public houses were demolished, some new ones being built with the former names.

The Victorian and Edwardian school buildings were demolished and replaced by smaller, lighter ones such as Huntingdon Primary School.

Although some of the ethnic minorities in St Ann's had their own religious buildings, these were mainly converted from existing buildings. The mosque on St Ann's Well Road was a new building in its own style.

In parts of the City centre, new buildings were sometimes built on the sites of older ones, sometimes with modern constructional features which did not blend with adjoining ones, as in Castle Gate.

Lawrence House on Clarendon Street was completed in 1973 in time for the re-organised City Council to house its technical staff there.

The loss of part of the swimming facilities at the older Victoria Baths in the 1970s was offset by the newly erected Beechdale Swimming Centre.

In addition to St Ann's, the Meadows also underwent redevelopment and a new building was the smaller St Patrick's Roman Catholic Church which replaced the much larger church of the same name on Canal Street.

The highway relocation in the Meadows allowed new light industry units, including this one on Castle Park industrial estate on Wilford Road.

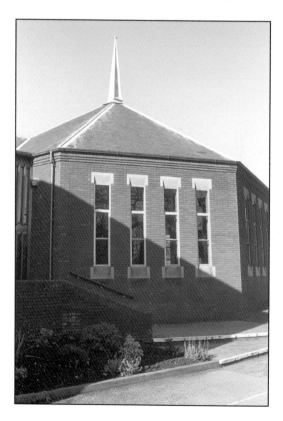

A modern contrast to Pugin's St Barnabas Cathedral is the Cathedral Hall built in the grounds, and designed by a Nottingham firm of architects, Eberlin and Partners.

Sovereign House on Nottingham Road, Basford is another example of the modern architecture of an industrial building, the vertical lines of the entrance blending with the horizontal cladding.

The building of Crabtree Farm Estate at Bulwell was followed by a radical re-alignment of the street pattern around the Market Place. A new bus station has this leisure building adjoining it, with a singularly anonymous rear façade.

A rather more relaxed type of building nearby at Bulwell reflects the modern trend of creating Job Centres in contrast to the standard government employment exchanges.

A new Bluecoat School on Aspley Lane replaced the Victorian building on Mansfield Road.

The 1970s saw the gradual replacement of Nottingham's temporary pre-fabricated bungalows. Some were demolished, whilst others were converted into permanent bungalows, like this one in Luton Close.

The Central Market on King Edward Street was built in 1926 to replace the market in the centuries old market place. When Victoria Centre was built, provision for an indoor market was included. The old one was demolished and the site used for new buildings such as these offices on Glasshouse Street.

A new building between Stoney Street and St Mary's Gate has a covered car park and offices. Its style was well designed to match that of the Lace Market.

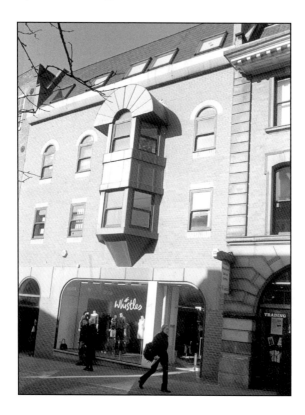

A new building on Middle Pavement was sandwiched between two existing units, with an attempt to match their Georgian façades.

A better example of a new building in a style sympathetic to its neighbours without copying exactly is Barclays House on Park Row erected in the 1990s.

The operation of a one-way traffic system up Derby Road was capped with a pleasant oasis at Canning Circus.

The last two decades of the twentieth century saw a gradual transformation of the redundant railway lands on the south side of Nottingham Canal. An out-of-town retail park on the historic King's Meadows was completed with a new bridge over the canal.

The north side of Talbot Street from Canning Circus to Clarendon Street has been almost wholly redeveloped in the last thirty years or so. Most recently has been the building of a Christian Centre.

Adjoining the Christian Centre on Talbot Street are a number of office blocks, home to various government departments.

Turney's leather factory has been converted into flats. The surrounding former industrial site has also been turned into a small secluded estate, with views over Nottingham Canal and the River Trent. The whole is now known as Turney's Quay.

Taken from Chaucer Street, this view shows some of the new buildings erected in recent years for Trent Polytechnic, now Nottingham Trent University. They occupy a large area between Chaucer Street and Goldsmith Street, as well as others in the vicinity.

Huntingdon Street former GPO sorting office was vacated some years ago and these new buildings were erected on an adjoining site on Lower Parliament Street.

This new block of offices is on Woodborough Road, between Mansfield Road and Huntingdon Street. The design has attracted favourable comment.

A few years ago, hooliganism on football grounds was a serious problem. To combat this, the Government and the football authorities embarked on a scheme to make all seating enclosures. The picture shows how Notts. County transformed its Meadow Lane ground.

The size of the St Ann's redevelopment meant that it had to be spread over a number of years. One of the last phases on Woodborough Road, below Cranmer Street, took advantage of the sloping site to produce a block of flats, Cheverton Court, with a series of stepped roofs. This has now been demolished.

Nearby, Maple Square was not successful. Built as a neighbourhood shopping centre, its failure to compete with the major shopping areas nearby has meant that it faces redevelopment and most of the buildings have now been demolished.

On Cranmer Street, the sloping site was used to good effect with Highwood House, an innovative scheme by the City Council for homeless families.

When a shop at the corner of Pelham Street and Clumber Street was demolished, a new building arose with a distinctly modern appearance. Good use of the corner to give a rounded entrance helps to soften the functional adjoining windows.

A public house, The Spinning Jenny, on the edge of the redeveloped Meadows area, did not prove successful. After demolition, the site was used to build a police station.

The former Scala Cinema on Market Street was converted to a public house before it was demolished. The new building was designed to replicate the appearance to some extent of the previous building.

The group of shops on Upper Parliament Street were built as recently as the 1970s, but have been given a facelift recently when the glazed first floor was added. The large office block to the rear was erected at the same time and extends to Wollaton Street.

To alleviate the traffic problem to some extent, a railway from Nottingham to Bulwell, which had only been for freight for 30 years, was adapted for passenger use. A new station was built and the route, at first only as far as Newstead, was later extended to Worksop. The Robin Hood Line is part of the County Council's effort to keep cars off the road.

Two railway lines formerly ran parallel to each other eastwards towards Carlton. One has now been converted to a road and the adjoining land used partly for new housing at Sneinton.

After a contentious proposal to build a new concert hall in the Lace Market area, the City Council decided instead to create a Royal Centre. This consisted of a refurbished Theatre Royal, the demolition of the former Empire Music Hall and the building of the new Concert Hall. This has proved to be an important step forward in Nottingham's place in the entertainment sphere.

The last 20 pictures of this chapter show only part of the City's transformation in the last decade of the twentieth century and must rank as the most extensive change in the City's history. An area between Talbot Street and Chaucer Street has seen the erection of several new modern buildings, including the Belgrave Centre, Nottingham Trent University's Law School.

The picture at the foot of page 20 shows the front and side elevation of New Castle House, formerly Viyella House. The rear elevation has been refurbished in this view from Nottingham Canal.

One of the most controversial schemes put forward was redevelopment of the former railway lands on the south bank of Nottingham Canal and Wilford Street. This was for a new Inland Revenue office and the original plans were strongly objected to. As a result, a competition for a new design was invited from six internationally known architects. The winning design from Sir Michael Hopkins and Partners has a number of towers which are functional as well as decorative.

Both sides of Nottingham Canal between Carrington Street and Wilford Street have been redeveloped. On the north side are new public houses with waterside outside seating areas, offices and the replacement offices of the Evening Post Group's headquarters from Forman Street.

On the south of the canal are Nottinghamshire Magistrates Court and Nottinghamshire Archives, now linked with the north side by a new footbridge.

The north bank of the canal westwards from Wilford Street has had new developments with offices and residential blocks between Castle Boulevard and the canal.

An interesting architectural feature can be seen on Clarendon Street, where a modern building has been built between two early twentieth century former school buildings. The Djanogly building is another part of Nottingham Trent University.

Part of Victoria Centre, at the corner of Mansfield Road and Union Road, has been tidied up by the erection of a national store.

The former bus station at the north end of Victoria Centre has given way to an extension of the shopping mall. A new bus station has been built on York Street.

Following the extension of the shopping mall, the Victoria Centre car park has been extended into the space which existed between Union Road and Woodborough Road. For thirty years, this space still showed the bed of the old Victoria Station after the railway lines and platforms had been removed.

Following the erection of the Nottingham University Teaching Hospital, the Queen's Medical Centre, the General Hospital site has seen refurbishment of parts and demolition of others. New office buildings shown here have been built on Standard Hill.

The drill hall at the rear of the Territorial Army's building on Derby Road has been demolished and this residential block built by a Housing Association.

The picture at the foot of page 23 showed the building erected in 1936 in Shakespeare Street for the Young Women's Christian Association. The Association has now moved to a new building on Colville Street.

The Queen's Golden Jubilee in 1997 has been commemorated in a new campus for the University of Nottingham. The Jubilee Campus on a former Raleigh Industries site on Ilkeston Road has the unusually shaped Information Technology building alongside a lake.

Some of the existing warehouses in the Lace Market have been converted to other uses, including residential and leisure. Between Hollowstone and Malin Hill, this new complex of flats, shops and offices has been built.

On the Ropewalk, the former Pay Bed wing of the General Hospital has been demolished and new apartments built in a style which harmonises with the Regency appearance of its neighbours.

An area of St Anns between Woodborough Road and Peas Hill Road had been left with existing industrial buildings. These had become something of a problem and have been demolished. The small group of bungalows has been built at the south end of Anforth Street.

This recently erected building on the east side of Maid Marian Way adjoining St James Street has an unusual system of windows as the central part of the frontage.

Nottingham's 1930s Ice Stadium has been demolished and a much larger National Ice Centre erected on its site and other adjoining sites. It was able to begin operating in the final year of the twentieth century.

Another large new building, The Cornerhouse on the cleared site of the former Nottingham Evening Post building, was not completed by the end of the twentieth century. A small part, T.G.I. Friday's, did manage to finish by a short head in December 2000.

# *Arnold*

When Urban District Councils were set up in 1895, Arnold was the largest in acreage of the five districts which adjoined the borough of Nottingham. Its 4,670 acres included 2,280 acres which were part of Sherwood Forest until they were enclosed in the late eighteenth century. This northern part was in 1901 almost entirely rural, as it is indeed still today.

The topography was rather unusual, as Arnold stretched for five miles from north to south, with a width seldom exceeding two miles. Its southern-most point was only two and a half miles from the centre of Nottingham and most of the inhabited part in 1901 was contained in a small area of about 120 acres between Furlong Street and High Street. This was a narrow strip running north to south, about a quarter of a mile wide. There was also a smaller, newer settlement at Daybrook to the south. The population of the urban district was 8,757, which was nearly double the figure for 30 years earlier.

Like many other small villages in the East Midlands, Arnold had grown in the early nineteenth century because of the growth of the hosiery and lace industries. The early growth was mainly in domestic or small workshop premises, but the last thirty years had seen the establishment of larger power-driven factories. In addition, Arnold had benefitted from increased employment opportunities with the building of a large brewery, soap works, laundry and two collieries in adjoining villages. In addition, two railways had joined together in this period with a station at Daybrook, which, along with new industrial premises, led to a growth in population.

The first two decades of the twentieth century saw a similar pattern of growth, with an increase in population of 3,000. A number of public buildings, including a library and two cinemas, were erected in this period, as well as a tram service to Nottingham. None of these survived, some have been replaced. Also at this time, a new suburb stretching from the city boundary to Thackeray's Lane grew up with more expensive housing. This part also started to grow eastwards towards Mapperley.

The following two decades saw a resumption of growth of population following the end of the 1914–18 War. A new feature was the building of council houses for the working classes, at low densities and with better facilities than the existing older houses. The main industries continued to flourish, with the exception of lace, but newer lighter industries took their place. Here, as in the rest of Britain, these stemmed from innovations such as the increased ownership of cars and radios as well as new modern cinemas and petrol omnibuses.

The Second World War prevented any large-scale development in the decade after 1945, apart from increased emphasis on building council houses. The last twenty five years of the Urban District Council saw a number of improvements in the town, including the demolition of most of the houses built in the previous century. The closing of the railway at Daybrook enabled redevelopment to take place at the southern end of the town.

By 1971, the population had grown to 33,254 and an estimated 35,000 in 1974, housed in 2,512 council houses and 10,268 private houses. Although some newer industries such as services were established, most of the district had become mainly residential with the growth of commuting. This pattern has continued with the absorption of Arnold into Gedling Borough Council. The last quarter of the century has seen much alteration of Arnold, with the virtual disappearance of the old centre of 1901. It has in its place received new amenities and modernisation, and at the same time has witnessed the disappearance of its industrial base. In its place, Arnold has become an important retail centre serving the town and surrounding district.

One of the first new buildings of the twentieth century was a new Baptist Chapel on Cross Street replacing an earlier one.

'The Ernehale' public house on Nottingham Road was opened in 1999, having been converted from former shops. The name is as given in Domesday Book as the forerunner of Arnold, meaning 'eagles nook or corner' in Old English. The date 1904 marked the erection of the first shop for Nottingham Co-operative Society.

A new residential suburb of Arnold was created in the decade from 1903. This was completely detached from the rest of the town, lying between Thackeray's Lane and the boundary of the district, Woodthorpe Drive. The houses were expensive, as the earliest ones on Villiers Road show.

The Urban District Council took early action under the Housing Act 1919 by building council houses, intended mainly for men with families who had served in the 1914–1918 War. These houses are on what was Arnold Hill Road, which was later changed to Arnot Hill Road.

In1923, the Home Brewery Company Limited built the Apollo Table Water factory on Mansfield Road. This was demolished recently and the date plaque was re-erected in the car park of Sainsbury's supermarket.

In the 1930s, the Home Brewery rebuilt its premises on Mansfield Road. The picture shows the rear view, the central stack being added later. When the brewery closed, the building was bought by Notts. County Council for offices.

In 1935, King George V celebrated the Silver Jubilee of his reign. To commemorate this, a national campaign was set up to provide playing fields throughout the country. Arnold recreation ground was laid out on Hallam's Lane.

King George VI's coronation took place in 1937 and this block of shops on Mansfield Road took its name accordingly.

The United Reformed Church building on Calverton Road was erected in 1938 on a site adjoining an earlier building. Originally known as a Congregational Church, the name was changed in the 1960s as were most of the others of the same denomination. The hall is a much more recent addition.

The Daybrook Laundry established in the 1880s had new buildings erected in the 1930s in a distinctly modern style.

Another building erected in 1938 was the Vale public house on Thackeray's Lane near the city boundary. Its distinctive style of architecture has survived both externally and internally.

In 1948, the East Midlands Electricity Board was created. The Board used existing premises for a time but in the 1970s built new premises on Coppice Road. These have been demolished and houses erected on the cleared site.

This view, taken from the junction of Rolleston Drive and Howbeck Road shows the extent of housing development northwards. The recreation ground on Killisick Road can be seen on the left of the picture.

One aspect of modern living is the growing preference for bungalows. Arnold now has its fair share, as shown in this picture, which also shows the gradients in the northern part.

In 1967, a new Arnold Methodist Church was built on Front Street on the site of an earlier church. The distinctive modern style was completely different from the three churches which were amalgamated in the new one.

The south end of Front Street was pedestrianised and a market place provided next to the new Methodist Church.

The pedestrianisation was completed at the junction with High Street by an area with trees and flower containers, which establishes itself as a gateway to Arnold with a welcome sign.

In the 1960s, the Nottingham City and Nottinghamshire County Fire Services were combined. The new authority's headquarters were built on Rolleston Drive but are now at Bestwood Lodge. The buildings on Rolleston Drive are now used for the County Council's Trading Standards Department.

Daybrook had a railway line and station with a bridge over Mansfield Road, just south of Daybrook Square. The line was one of the victims of the Beeching cuts and the bridge and station were demolished. The site has been developed as a retail park.

A number of the public houses in Arnold have names associated with Sherwood Forest. The Arrow on Gedling Road is one of them, the present ornate building replacing an earlier one.

The Salvation Army has had a presence in Arnold for over a hundred years and has recently had a building erected on High Street which provides for its various activities.

Most of the buildings in the older part of Arnold between High Street and Front Street were demolished from 1960 onwards. At the northern end, Arnold Leisure Centre was opened in 1982 and has a swimming pool, theatre and library.

Arnold Hill Park and Hall were acquired in 1913 by the Urban District Council. When Gedling District was formed in 1974, its headquarters were at Carlton. In 1976, new offices were built adjoining the park in pleasant landscaped surroundings.

The loss of the Home Brewery and the future of its site led to a great deal of concern by Arnold's residents. Fortunately, the landmark main building was spared and demolition of other buildings has led to the construction of a new road, Sir John Robinson's Way, and a supermarket.

# Beeston

*Wright's Directory of Nottingham* for 1902 described Beeston as an extensive, populous and improving township. Its population in 1901 at 8,960 was almost three times that of 1851. The Urban District Council formed in 1895 only covered the parish of Beeston of 1,601 acres. It was the smallest but the most industrialised of the five urban districts created around Nottingham. It had been an industrial village in the early nineteenth century when it had over 100 bobbin net machines, stocking frames and a silk mill employing 200 workmen.

When the first railway line from Nottingham to Derby was built in 1839, Beeston had a station on the line between the old village and the River Trent. This must have contributed to Beeston's later industrial growth. In 1901, it had lace and hosiery factories, an iron foundry, maltings, breweries, a creosote works for dipping railway sleepers and, most important of all, the Humber Company, then employing 1800 workers.

The manufacturers and managerial staff must have comprised a substantial middle class proportion of the population. The 1901 edition of the Ordnance Survey map shows an interesting housing development to the west of the village. This was part of a Freehold Land Society. Described as Belle Vue Park and St John's Grove, the street pattern clearly indicated the planned layout. The houses, mainly detached, were then few in number but later filled up to create a new suburb. The St John's Grove area consisted of about three acres bounded by Denison Street, Imperial Road, Chilwell Road and Devonshire Avenue, which still retains its purely residential character.

The population of Beeston increased by a relatively modest amount between 1901 and 1911, due mainly to the removal of the Humber factory to Coventry, which reputedly left 600 empty houses. The establishment of the National Telephone Company, later to join with L. M. Ericsson of Stockholm, helped to provide employment and, by 1921, the population had risen to 12,494.

The 1920s saw two factors influence further growth. First was the building of council houses and, second, the establishment of the University College of Nottingham just over the City border. This would have created a modest amount of employment opportunities and trade.

The 1930s were to be a period when considerable changes took place. When the boundaries of the urban districts were reviewed in 1934, Beeston and

Stapleford U.D.C. was created by adding Bramcote, Chilwell, Stapleford and Toton to result in an area of 6,462 acres and a population of 27,812. In addition, the telephone company Ericssons continued to grow, employing 4,500 by 1939, whilst the Boots Company in 1929 started a move away from the City of Nottingham to a site partly in Beeston and partly in the City.

The creation of the expanded urban district was marked by the erection of a new town hall, but the Second World War prevented normal development for six years, apart from the expansion of Chilwell Ordnance Depot.

After the War, the first priority was the building of new council houses, and some private ones for the first ten years or so. By 1961, the population had risen to 32,000 and ten years later to more than 56,000. New industries were established and some of the established ones, especially Boots, expanded. The granting of University status to the former College and its subsequent expansion, although mainly in the city, attracted staff and some students as residents.

The final years of the Urban District saw a number of changes in the appearance of the town, clearance of older houses, highway improvements, redevelopment of The Square and pedestrianisation of shopping streets.

A noteworthy feature throughout the post-war period has been the transformation of land adjoining the River Trent, with the cessation of quarrying followed by the creation of Attenborough Nature Reserve.

The creation of Broxtowe District Council, now designated a Borough with a Mayor, has resulted in its building a new headquarters to supplement the former Town Hall. Other developments have been in the provision of leisure facilities and the building of warden-aided blocks of flats. Two recent developments reflecting late twentieth-century progress have been a technology park and a new Royal Mail sorting office equipped with electronic machinery, which has replaced former offices in the City.

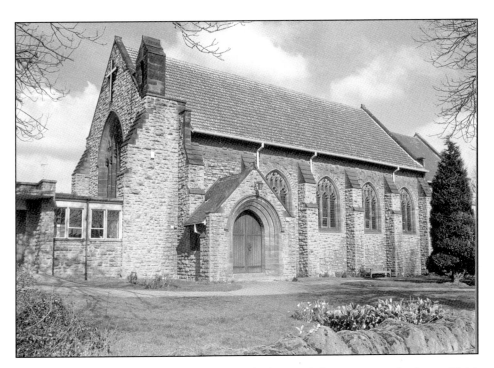

One of the first buildings to be erected in Beeston in the twentieth century was what is now Christ Church on Chilwell Road. It was built as a mission church to St Mary's, Attenborough, in which parish Chilwell then was. It was consecrated as a separate church in 1912.

Another religious building in 1902 was a new Methodist Church, also on Chilwell Road but in Beeston itself. Designed by a Bradford architect, it is distinguished by its tall spire.

This pair of houses has the date stone 1902. They are typical of the better standard of houses built in late Victorian and Edwardian periods, especially the industrial houses in terraces of earlier years.

A rather larger house in Station Road has distinctive features. It was built by John H. Brough, a well-known Beeston builder, as his own residence.

An example of early philanthropy is the Beeston Lads' Club building on Station Road, erected in 1913 with funds provided by a well-known local businessman, S. H. Pearson.

A major addition to Chilwell was the munitions factory built during the First World War. The site was greatly expanded during and after the Second World War as a garrison and Ordnance Depot.

Regent Hall on the south side of Station Road was built in the 1920s by John H. Brough (see page 80). The ground floor was used as a garage, the upper floor being used as a dance hall up to 1939.

The new Town Hall on Foster Avenue was built in 1938 as headquarters of the newly expanded area named Beeston and Stapleford Urban District Council.

Twenty five years later, work commenced on a site adjoining the Town Hall on a new Roman Catholic Church of St Peter.

The final years of the Urban District Council were accompanied by demolition of older properties around The Square and highway alterations to provide a new precinct.

Increased use of buses through Beeston was met by a new bus station with a shopping mall leading to The Square.

Recent years have seen the building of complexes for the elderly, such as Grove Court on Bramcote Avenue.

The statue of a beekeeper on High Road was inspired by the one-time widespread occupation of beekeeping in Beeston (or is it a play on its name?).

A new Post Office has been erected on a site adjoining the old one in Chilwell Road. A new public house on the site of the old one has been appropriately named.

The increased status of the Borough of Broxtowe has been accompanied by the erection of new offices opposite the Town Hall.

The new council has provided new leisure facilities such as Bramcote Baths on Derby Road.

Housing development has spread westwards into Chilwell without too much intrusion into the green belt.

Other housing spreading northwards towards Beeston Fields golf course includes these half-timbered gabled houses on Larch Crescent.

A pleasant footpath separates housing from the golf course beyond Cator Lane.

South of the railway station, a former cricket ground and bowling green has become the site of a technology business park.

A site associated with communications businesses throughout the century now has adjoining it Plessey Business Park, seen here from Nelson Street.

Smaller light industries sites have also been established like this one on Nether Street.

The new buildings labelled Broxtowe College are part of De Montfort University on the site of the former Beeston College of Further Education on Chilwell High Road.

The new Royal Mail sorting office on Padge Road, built to replace former offices in Nottingham, emphasises Beeston's role as part of Greater Nottingham.

# *Carlton*

When Carlton was made an Urban District in 1894, it was the only such district of the five adjacent to the Borough of Nottingham which was divided into wards: Carlton, Porchester and Netherfield. This reflected the different topography of its area compared to the other four districts. Carlton itself – its proper name being Carlton in the Willows, to distinguish it from the other Carltons in the county – was only created as a separate ecclesiastical parish in 1883. Prior to that date, it had been part of the ecclesiastical parish of Gedling. In 1891, the latter had a population of only 520, compared with Carlton's 4,546.

By 1831, Carlton already had four times the population of Gedling, at 1,704 inhabitants. It had grown, like the other villages close to the Borough, because of the hosiery and lace trades. It had a long common boundary with the Borough, along what is now Porchester Road. Most of its inhabitants lived near the main road which climbed up from the old village centre to join the Borough's Carlton Road. Its industries also included a number of brickworks. The land fell steeply to the north-east to a valley and then rose again to what is now Westdale Lane. This part of the urban district, Porchester Ward, had grown from mainly agricultural land to a residential suburb in the last quarter of the nineteenth century. This started in 1886 by the purchase of 122 acres by a committee for the provision of allotments. Many of the allotment holders built sheds and summerhouses on them and, from about 1904, more permanent houses were built on some of the plots. Gradually the area developed as a residential suburb with new roads running between Porchester Road and Westdale Lane, as well as some leading south from the Plains. A small shopping centre made the area fairly self-sufficient for most everyday needs.

A similar development took place from the north side of Carlton Hill, with the result that the original Carlton village area spread into a sizeable urban district, for which a Local Board was established.

Netherfield was a fairly flat area between the main through road from Nottingham to Burton Joyce and beyond and extending south to the River Trent. Something of a physical barrier dividing the Carlton area were the two railway lines which ran more or less side by side from Nottingham. One was the Midland Railway line to Lincoln, whilst the other branched off at Netherfield to cross the River Trent.

It was the railway lines, and from the mid-1880s, a depot of the London and North Western Railway, which created Netherfield. Originally a small hamlet in the adjoining parish of Colwick, it became an industrial area with a large cotton doubling mill.

At the 1901 census, the population of the Urban District was 10,041. Most of the working inhabitants were employed by the railway companies, some hosiery factories and nearby Gedling Colliery. The frequent train services to Nottingham would also provide transport for employment there. The character of the district was not changed much for the next 50 years. Steady growth of population reaching 26,000 by 1931 and an estimated 30,000 by 1939 was met by the erection of new houses, including some council houses from 1920 onwards. There was a small increase in population from outside the original urban district area when Gedling and part of Colwick were added in 1934. This part of Colwick had changed in the 1920s when an industrial estate was formed. It was laid out with private roads, each known only by a number. The existence of the River Trent nearby resulted in a number of oil companies establishing depots which were supplied with oil by barges.

Although there was some increase in commercial and professional employment in the 1920s and '30s, such as motor car agents and garages, electrical concerns, banks, building societies and estate agents, there were no large industrial developments. Bus and later trolley bus services were added to the existing railway facilities which would enable increased employment outside the area.

The end of the War in 1945 saw a resumption of house building, both council and private. The 1960s changed the physical appearance of the centre of Carlton when older houses were demolished. By 1970 this area had a modern look to it. A tall office block was erected between Station Road and Burton Road for the Council Offices, whilst opposite was a multi-storey housing block. The area at the junction of Carlton Hill and Cavendish Road included a new superstore and other shopping facilities. Another new development in 1970 was the establishment of a large leisure complex, Carlton Forum, which incorporated outdoor sports facilities and indoor amenities, including a swimming pool.

The nationalisation of railway lines in the 1960s included the closing of one railway line from Nottingham, the former LNER line which ran parallel to the other line through Colwick. The line from Nottingham continues to Newark and Lincoln, still with the hold-ups to traffic from the level crossing. Trains for Grantham use the same line as far as Colwick before it branches off towards the River Trent, which it crosses. Another major development was the closing of the former London and North Western depot at Netherfield and Colwick Sidings. The former Nottingham to Gedling branch line has also disappeared.

This has meant a considerable change at the east side of Netherfield. At the same time, the former LNER line was converted to a road which bypasses Colwick, in a loop road. This has alleviated to some extent the traffic problem through central Carlton and has opened up land for new development. This includes a new retail and business park on the east side of the loop road, which also includes a new bridge over the railway line. Recent years have seen the disappearance of two major industrial employers, Gedling Colliery and Bourne's Mill at Netherfield. The site of the latter has been used for housing.

Since 1974, the former Urban District has become part of Gedling Borough. One of its most significant changes in Carlton has been in the leisure field. Carlton Forum has been refurbished and now occupies two sites and another centre, the Richard Herrod Bowles centre, has been built.

Carlton remains a mainly residential area and its nearness to the City for employment, shopping and as a cultural centre means that it becomes an integral part of the Greater Nottingham concept.

One of the first new public buildings of the twentieth century to be built in Carlton was the Free Library erected with assistance from the scheme set up by Andrew Carnegie, the Scottish born philanthropist.

Shops and a bank on Meadow Road, Netherfield erected about this time also showed some architectural style.

A cinema erected about 1912 was the Victoria Picture Palace on Station Road in a highly decorative style. The building is now used as a church.

Some of the houses built about the same time were of a superior type to most of the earlier working-class accommodation. This one at the junction of Station Road and Wallace Avenue is a good example, with first-class brickwork.

The valley between Carlton Hill and Westdale Lane was developed with housing starting early in the century and continuing throughout the remainder of the century.

The Post Office Telephone Exchange, as it was then known, on Station Road, was built to a standard pattern. It is now occupied by a textile firm.

The increase in population in the inter-war period led to the erection of new houses both by the Urban District Council and by private builders. Semi-deteached pairs such as the one on Redland Grove were the most popular.

The threat of war in the 1930s led to an increase in numbers of the Territorial Army and new drill halls were built, including this one on Cavendish Grove.

The development of new housing in the Porchster area led to the building of a new church on Marshall Hill Drive in 1938, dedicated to St James.

The nearness of the River Trent at Colwick led to an industrial estate being developed there from 1920 onwards. Oil tanks were fed from barges along the Humber and Trent.

The system of labour exchanges was expanded in the 1930s by providing purpose-built offices for payment of unemployment benefit. These were mainly of a standard pattern, like the one on Victoria Road, Netherfield.

The pre-war fire station on Gedling Road was demolished and replaced by a more modern one on an adjoining site on Station Road in the 1960s.

The residential suburb in the Porchester area was expanded northwards of Westdale Lane in the second half of the twentieth century. A new Baptist church was erected and later a community centre was built on an adjoining site.

The demolition of older unfit houses in the 1960s enabled redevelopment of the centre of Carlton. A large office block between Burton Road and Station Road dominated what was named Carlton Square.

On the south side of Station Road, a six-storey block of flats known as Walton Court complemented the opposite office block.

Main Street was renamed Carlton Hill and new buildings erected near the junction with Cavendish Road, including a supermarket.

Another building formerly on Main Street was demolished and a replacement built nearby. It retained its original name Windsor Castle (a public house).

A new police station was erected on Cavendish Road which had long since had its name changed from the original Cemetery Road.

After Carlton Urban District was absorbed in 1974 into Gedling District Council, the latter built a new leisure centre on Foxhill Road, Carlton Forum.

The closing of one of the two parallel railway lines led to it being made into a road which connected with a new loop road by passing Colwick and Netherfield.

The new loop road opened up land on either side for redevelopment, including a large retail park.

Modern ideas led to the abolition of labour exchanges and their replacement by Job Centres. The one on Victoria Road, Netherfield has a welcome sign and its own web-site reference.

New houses on Francis Road display modern fashions of windows and doorways.

A new industrial unit on the Colwick Industrial Estate has a commanding presence at the junction of two roads.

In 1990, Carlton Business Centre was erected by Gedling Borough Council on a site off Station Road, formerly used for a school. It consisted of 21 industrial units.

The boundary marker between Nottingham and Carlton, seen on the left. The street nameplate is dated 1877.

# *Hucknall*

Hucknall Torkard, which was still its official designation at the beginning of the twentieth century, was the most northerly of the five urban districts surrounding Nottingham which became separate councils in 1895. The town had a population of 15,250 at the 1901 census, which made it the largest of the five districts. From a population of 2,836 in 1861, it had grown to 10,023 by 1881. This was due mainly to the establishment of two collieries, Hucknall in 1861, followed by Linby. The latter place was and remained a small village and as the colliery was only a mile or so from Hucknall, most of its men would have lived there.

At the beginning of the century, about 2,000 men were employed at the two collieries, whilst another 500 people were employed in the hosiery and shawl-making trades. Another major concern was a cigar factory employing 400 people, mainly women. Employment was also available at Kirkby and Sutton in Ashfield as well as Nottingham, as all were connected by railways. Hucknall had three lines and four stations, the Great Central Railway having been opened at the start of the century. This line had 49 trains a day and it took only 13 or 14 minutes for passenger trains to reach Nottingham, which would offer employment, especially to women, in the lace trade.

Hucknall did not experience the growth of the middle classes in the first decade of the century, unlike Beeston and West Bridgford. Its population remained static in this period, a mere increase of 650 between the two censuses. This was no doubt due to the predominance of the mining industry. J. B. Firth described it in 1916 as 'a dreary mining town of depressing ugliness' in his book *Highways and Byways of Nottinghamshire.*

The two post-1918 decades saw some improvement in the appearance of the town. An early start was made in the building of council houses, as elsewhere, to a much improved standard. Private builders also contributed by building for owner-occupiers and clearing some of the worst central area older houses. By 1939, the population at 19,890 was only about a third more than in 1901, but the number of houses, 6,000, was double the figure of 40 years earlier.

The Urban District Council had members in this decade who were anxious to improve the quality of life in the town. Their efforts were hampered by economic conditions, particularly by the industrial strife in the 1920s, which particularly affected mining areas. Some assistance was forthcoming from private benefactors. The Council was able to lay out Titchfield Park on land given by the Duke of Portland and two other schemes were inaugurated by Sir Julien Cahn. These were an attractive group of almshouses opposite the park and an orthopaedic clinic.

The 1930s, especially the later years, saw some further progress with some modern factories being built and Rolls-Royce taking over the aerodrome which had been built during the First World War. This did not please everyone, some of those who lived near the airfield complaining of the noise. Another feature of the '30s was the opening of a new modern cinema, the Byron, which still functions as such.

The collieries and the aerodrome were essential to the war effort and, after the War, the mines which had been nationalised were improved by greater mechanisation. The early post-war years were marked by a renewal of council house building, and later by private house building which has continued.

Hucknall's narrow based economy was dealt two serious blows when the railways through the town felt the Beeching axe and the more recent closure and disappearance of the two collieries. Since 1974, Hucknall has been part of Ashfield District Council, which has continued the services provided by the former Urban District Council. As in the other districts, leisure facilities have been increased and housing for special needs, such as warden-aided accommodation, provided. A new bypass road south of the town has relieved the older central part of through traffic. The return of passenger trains, the Robin Hood Line from Nottingham to Worksop, includes use of a station at Hucknall. The end of the century has seen the start of the Nottingham Express Transit modern tram system, completed in 2004.

Beardall Street School was started in 1872 but was enlarged in 1901, extending to Duke Street. The doorway, windows and gable were more ornate than the usual school board architecture.

The Wesleyan Reform Church on Ogle Street was erected in 1906.

The area to the east of the railway line was developed in the early years of the twentieth century. The terrace of houses on Papplewick Lane were of a higher standard than most of Hucknall's earlier houses.

King Edward Street was laid out on a site off Watnall Road which was undeveloped at the beginning of the twentieth century.

Adjoining the houses is this more modern industrial building.

Hucknall Aerodrome was built during the 1914–1918 War and in the 1950s was developed by Rolls-Royce after the Royal Air Force moved out.

Titchfield Park was developed in the 1920s by the Urban District Council on land given by the Duke of Portland. The park-keeper's house is now unoccupied.

This delightful group of almshouses on Park Drive was erected by another wealthy benefactor, Julien Cahn, later created a knight and baronet. He lived at Papplewick Grange nearby and was famous for his own cricket eleven in the 1920s and 30s.

Park Drive and other adjacent areas were developed as a private estate in the 1920s with large detached houses.

One house on Park Drive was built in a completely different style to its neighbours, with its innovative flat roof.

Hucknall has been able to retain its art-deco Byron Cinema erected in 1938, although it has had to include the later alteration which has been the fate of other cinemas in the TV era.

The aerodrome's considerable contribution to the Second World War's aviation history is commemorated in the public house named after one of the aircraft born there.

The redevelopment of much of Hucknall's housing has seen the creation of flats and warden-aided complexes by Ashfield District Council.

Holy Cross Roman Catholic Church's first century-old building was demolished and replaced by a new one.

The modern style, low rise Holy Cross primary school is on Leen Mills Lane.

A modern housing estate has been built on the east side of the railway line extending as far as the border of Gedling Borough Council.

Another new housing estate on Linby Lane has large detached houses with plenty of green spaces.

The disappearance of the collieries and most of Hucknall's former railway lines has opened up new areas for development. The Robin Hood Line has been re-opened for passengers and the former colliery site on the east side of the line now has houses and light industry.

The post-war increase in the number of motor cars has led to the erection of garages such as the one on Papplewick Lane.

Another feature of recent years has been the setting up of health centres such as this one on Watnall Road.

The same road also has this new doctor's surgery.

A new small industrial estate has been built on Occupation Road.

Ashfield District Council, like the other new councils set up in 1974, has provided Hucknall with a new leisure centre on Linby Lane.

A new further education building on Portland Road is part of the recently formed consortium of such colleges under the title of New College Nottingham.

The Hucknall bypass section of the A611 road has not only helped to relieve the centre of the town of through traffic, but opened up areas for new building such as this industrial estate on Watnall Road near the junction with the bypass.

The Hucknall terminus of the tram, now fully operational, is next to the Robin Hood line from Nottingham to Worksop.

# West Bridgford

At the beginning of the twentieth century, West Bridgford was one of the five urban districts created in 1895. It was the smallest of them both in acreage and population. It was also the only one of the five which was not an industrial area. From a village in 1881, with a population of 250, it had grown in population to 2,500 in 1891 and to 7,018 in 1901. This rapid growth was due to a planned decision of the major land-owner to establish a residential suburb. The newly built houses on the principal through roads had by covenant to be of a specified minimum size and value. Most of its residents in 1901 were families who had come to live in West Bridgford from Nottingham and nearby areas. The heads of families were either owners of manufacturing businesses, professional men, owners of retail shops or highly-paid employees. Few of these worked in West Bridgford.

The area had its own school board first elected in 1895 and had two schools, one on Musters Road and the other on Trent Boulevard. Most of the houses in 1901 were near to Trent Bridge, from the City side of which public transport was available. Part of West Bridgford to the east of the Grantham Canal had started to develop only in 1892 and still had relatively few houses in 1901. The parish church of St. Giles had been enlarged in 1898 and there were three non-conformist chapels, two Wesleyan Methodists and one Congregational.

The first two decades saw continued expansion of population from elsewhere and of dwellings to house them. The population in 1914 was more than double, at 17,476, that of 1901. There were few other buildings erected during this period. Among those that were was a headquarters for Urban District Council in 1907, a Masonic Hall in 1912, two fire stations and a council depot. The town already had a public house, the Trent Bridge Inn, adjoining the Notts County Cricket Club's ground, but a strong non-conformist body successfully opposed the granting of licences for new ones until 1936. Even the offer for the town to have a Carnegie library was refused on the grounds that the residents could afford to buy their own books.

Growth resumed after the First World War, but mainly in housing to accommodate a continued increase in population. There was still no sizeable industry, apart from a laundry. The Urban District Council elections were held on a Monday so that the commercial travellers could vote before they commenced their journeys. The inter-war period saw an expansion of facilities mainly for the resident population. A public park, library, shopping centres and recreational facilities were features.

The period also saw two unsuccessful attempts by the City Council to bring West Bridgford within the City boundary. 1935 saw the Urban District's area tripled by the inclusion of Edwalton and Wilford. This had little effect on the town at that time because of the outbreak of war in 1939. After the war, building of new houses resumed, including estates in the two parishes absorbed. In 1952, a boundary alteration resulted in the part of Wilford west of the former Great Central railway line being transferred to the City of Nottingham. At the same time, the boundary with the City around Trent Bridge was altered so lands south of the bridge, which had for centuries been part of the Borough, were transferred to the county and to West Bridgford Urban District. A major feature of this was the transfer of Nottingham Forest's football ground, still called the City Ground, and the site and building of the new County Hall became part of the Urban District. The County Hall, which had been started before the 1939–45 War, had to remain mainly unfinished during the war. It was several years before it was finally completed and the County Council's headquarters transferred from its former premises on High Pavement.

Post-war housing development took place to the south of the district, at Wilford Hill and Edwalton. A notable addition to the district's recreational facilities was the acquisition by the Urban District Council of the former cricket ground on Loughborough Road. This had been owned by the wealthy Sir Julien Cahn, who had his own cricket team. The ground was restored and improved after years of wartime neglect and renamed West Park.

Another change, again on Loughborough Road, was the erection of one of the country's first supermarkets. Opened in 1964 as the GEM, it was later renamed ASDA and, following a large extension, became a hypermarket owned by an American retail organisation.

Most of the town's Victorian and Edwardian residences still remain, although many of the larger ones have been converted into flats or offices and, in quite a number, to use as nursing homes or retirement homes. With the continued growth of villages in the south of the county, traffic has increased to such an extent that major changes to the roads system have had to be made. The A52 road has been diverted to the south, to cross the Trent by Clifton Bridge, and the former railway line bridge at Lady Bay has been converted to a road bridge. Trent Bridge and its approaches have been altered to cope with increased traffic.

In 1974, the Urban District became part of Rushcliffe Borough and West Bridgford was chosen as the Council's headquarters, with its offices in a former hotel. Leisure and recreational facilities have seen major expansion. The Council has built two leisure centres, one with a swimming pool and the other with an indoor bowls centre, and the two major sporting venues, City Ground and Trent Bridge Cricket Ground, have been transformed into modern stadia. Two additional parishes have been created, each with their own church, a Further

Education College has been built and a new Police Divisional Headquarters, Ambulance and Fire Stations have also been built.

At the end of the twentieth century, West Bridgford is still primarily residential without manufacturing industry. The changes in the last quarter of the century have added other aspects to its character, many of which have created employment opportunities. As the town is nearer to the centre of Nottingham than most parts of the city, its development as part of Greater Nottingham was probably more significant than the other districts. Its separation from the City administratively, due to the presence of the River Trent, was something the City Council in particular considered anomalous.

Some of the earliest houses to be erected in the twentieth century were detached houses to individual designs, such as this one on Musters Road.

A link with the City of Nottingham was the construction of a suspension bridge upstream from Trent Bridge. Designed primarily to carry a new water main for the city's waterworks, it also served as a footbridge for pedestrians.

The growth in the number of middle class businessmen in the first decade resulted in the building of a Masonic hall on the West Bridgford side near the suspension bridge.

The Urban District Council met in schoolrooms until 1907 when it built a new headquarters at 8 Bridgford Road. This later became a bank and is now a twenty-four hour store.

After the First World War, new housing development started south of Melton Road. The houses were usually smaller than the large houses built earlier and this semi-detached pair on Eton Road is typical.

In 1923, St Giles Church had a new parochial hall built on Church Drive. The building is now owned by Rushcliffe Borough Council as a community hall used for a variety of purposes.

In 1925 a widening of Trent Bridge was started and this involved taking buildings down at the corner of Radcliffe Road. After the widening was completed, new buildings were erected, including shops with flats above and a bank, in two contrasting styles.

After the Urban Council acquired The Hall, a reading room was provided in it. In 1939, a new County Library was opened on land adjoining the park which had been acquired with The Hall.

For forty years, applications for public house licences were refused but in 1936 two were granted. One on Gordon Road was intended to be the Rushcliffe Hotel, but its nearness to Trent Bridge cricket ground influenced a change to the Test Match.

In 1936, a start was made on building a new headquarters for Notts. County Council on a site formerly used as sports grounds. The Second World War and post-war economic difficulties prevented completion of the original plan until 1963. Extensions at the south end have been added since.

A large house on Loughborough Road was built as one of the first houses on the road by John Rushworth, after whom the adjoining avenue is named. It was demolished about 1938 and a new block of flats, Rushworth Court, was built on the site.

One of the earliest post-1946 buildings other than houses was a new school on Musters Road, named after a former headmaster and councillor, Jesse Gray. It represented a complete contrast to the style of the earliest Bridgford schools. A playing field adjoins the school.

The modern flats built after the Second World War on Fox Road have balconies with a view of Trent Bridge Cricket Ground.

Another early post-war development was the ambulance station on Rectory Road, with its distinctive doors.

The last of the former farm houses at the corner of Rectory Road and Bridgford Road was demolished in the 1960s and a new telephone exchange erected on the site.

Almost opposite the telephone exchange was The Poplars, which had been built in the first decade of the nineteenth century for the Hornbuckle family. It was demolished in 1960 and replaced by a block of flats with the same name.

This stretch of road from Radcliffe Road to Rutland Road was built in 1953 to replace a swing bridge which formerly allowed traffic along the Grantham Canal. It was known as the Meccano bridge from its appearance.

The site between Albert Road and Davies Road at Tudor Square was cleared of older buildings and the bank and shops erected in the 1960s.

The only high-rise building in West Bridgford so far is Trent Bridge House at the corner of Radcliffe Road and Fox Road. It was built in the mid-1970s for departments of Notts. County Council.

A feature of the latter part of the twentieth century was the increase in the number of dwellings erected and managed by Housing Associations. This block, known as Peveril Court, was built about 1980 at the corner of Melton Road and Musters Road.

The police station on Rectory Road, erected in the 1930s, was demolished as well as the adjoining rectory to provide the site for a new divisional headquarters of the Nottinghamshire Police Authority.

Nottingham Forest football club's home, City Ground, was gradually transformed during the 1990s as an all-seat stadium with other facilities.

The ubiquitous big M chain of restaurants even made its appearance on Radcliffe Road.

The 1990s saw the gradual expansion of housing on the west side of Wilford Hill to form a distinct new estate, of larger, more expensive houses, known as Compton Acres, with its own shopping precinct.

The last year of the twentieth century saw the completion of a radical change to Central Avenue by limiting vehicular access to buses and access to shops during the daytime.